AMAZING ANIMAL BODIES

Stingers

ANNE ACCARDI

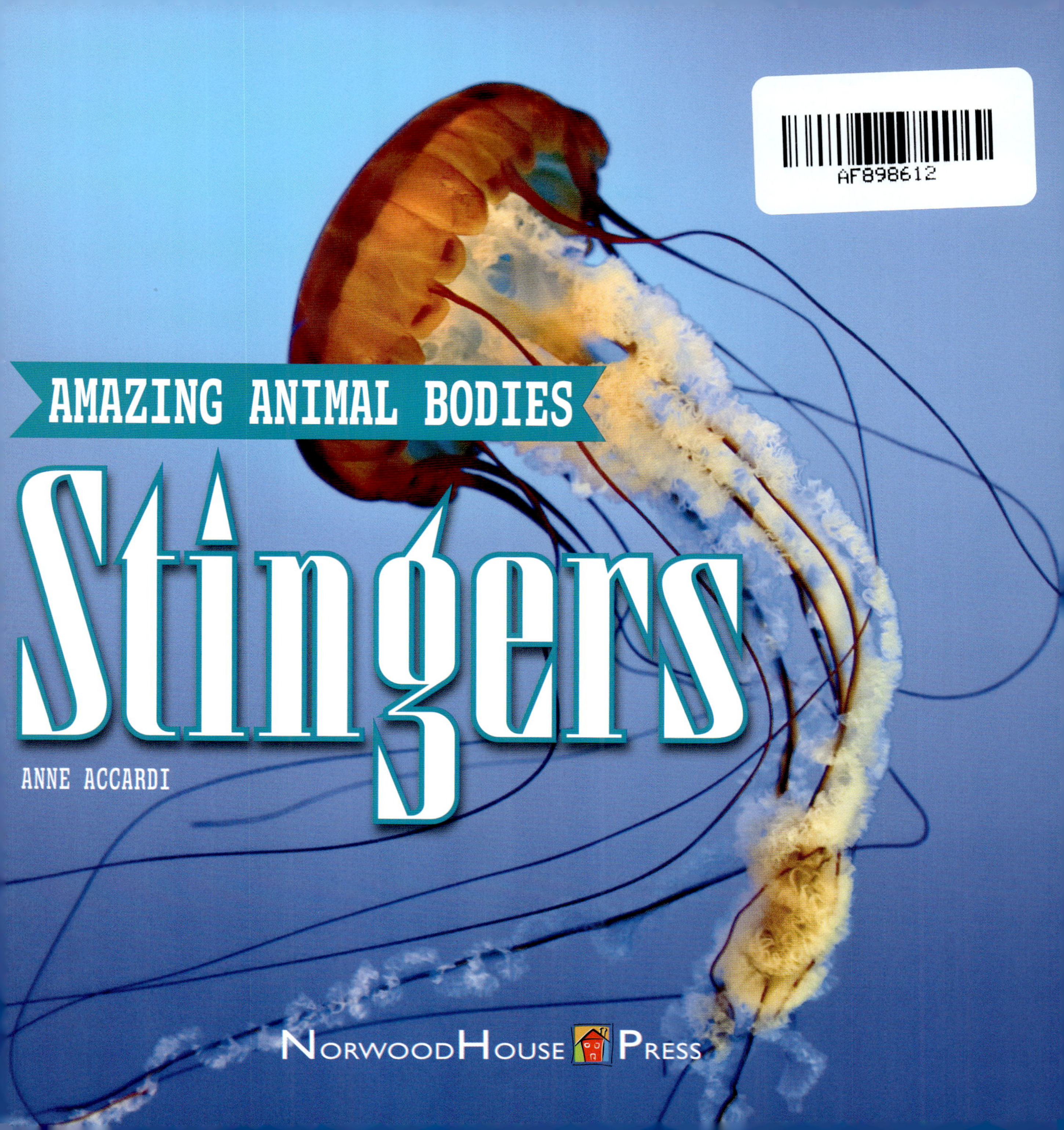

NORWOOD HOUSE PRESS

Cataloging-in-Publication Data

Names: Accardi, Anne.
Title: Stingers / Anne Accardi.
Description: Buffalo, NY : Norwood House Press, 2027. | Series: Amazing animal bodies | Includes glossary and index.
Identifiers: ISBN 9781978579576 (pbk.) | ISBN 9781978579583 (library bound) | ISBN 9781978579590 (ebook)
Subjects: LCSH: Animal defenses--Juvenile literature. | Bites and stings--Juvenile literature.
Classification: LCC QL759.A33 2027 | DDC 591.47--dc23

Published in 2027 by
Norwood House Press
2544 Clinton Street
Buffalo, NY 14224

Designer: Rhea Magaro
Editor: Kim Thompson

Photo credits: Cover, p. 1 Baishev/Shutterstock.com; p. 5 Wirestock Creators/Shutterstock.com; p. 6 Katho Menden/Shutterstock.com; p. 7 Frank Reiser/Shutterstock.com; p. 9 Amam ka/Shutterstock.com; p. 10 Lakshan LG/Shutterstock.com; p. 11 Ilya Andriyanov/Shutterstock.com; p. 13 Bachkova Natalia/Shutterstock.com; p. 14 Henk Bouma/Shutterstock.com; p. 15 Witsawat.S/Shutterstock.com; p. 16 RB Punnad/Shutterstock.com; p. 17 Vijin Varghese/Shutterstock.com; p. 18 Allexxandar/Shutterstock.com; p. 21 mc_pongsatorn/Shutterstock.com;

Printed in the United States of America

CPSIA compliance information: Batch #CSNHP27: For further information contact Norwood House Press at 1-800-237-9932.

TABLE OF CONTENTS

What Are Stingers? 4
Bee Stingers 10
Wasp Stingers 12
Ant Stingers 14
Scorpion Stingers 16
Stingray Stingers 19
Jellyfish Stingers 20
Glossary 22
Thinking Questions 23
Index 24
About the Author 24

What Are Stingers?

Stingers are sharp body parts. Many **insects** have them. Other animals have them too.

Stingers jab and stab. They sting enemies. They sting **prey**. They can sting people and pets.

Some stingers have **barbs**. They can only stab once. They cannot pull out to use again.

Stingers carry **venom**. It hurts!

Victims can itch. They can swell up.

They can die.

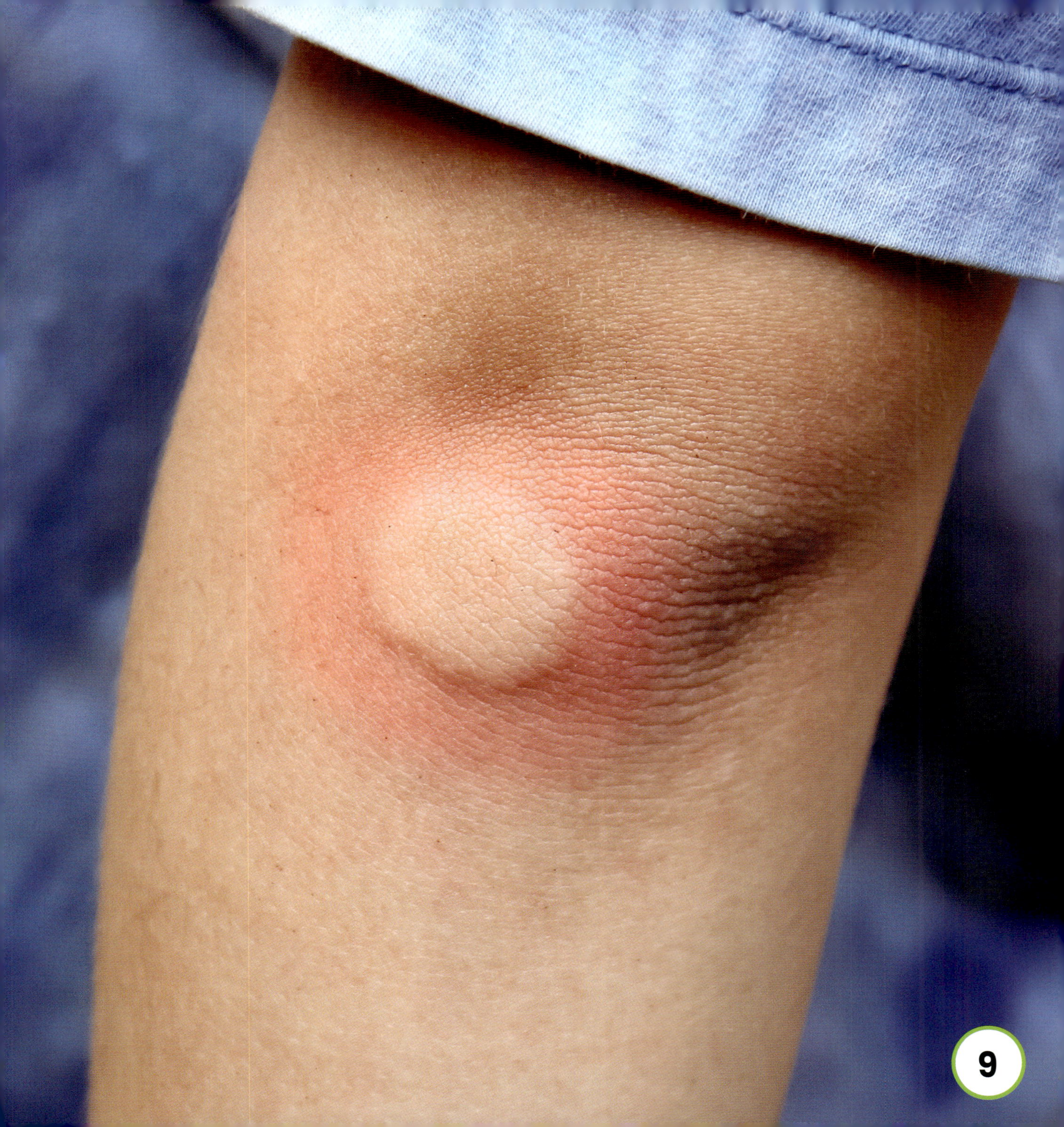

Bee Stingers

Bees sting. They sting to protect their **hives**.

Their stingers have barbs. If a bee stings, its skin rips. The bee dies.

Wasp Stingers

Wasps sting. Their stingers do not have barbs. They can sting many times.

Ant Stingers

Fire ants sting. They sting to **defend** their nests.

The sting hurts. It feels like fire!

Scorpion Stingers

Scorpions sting. They have stingers on their tails.

Their stingers are very sharp!

A sting can kill.

Stingray Stingers

Stingrays sting. Their tails have stingers. They look like spikes.

If a stingray is afraid, it will sting!

Jellyfish Stingers

Jellyfish sting. Their arms are called **tentacles**. They are covered in stingers.

Fish get stung. Jellyfish eat them up!

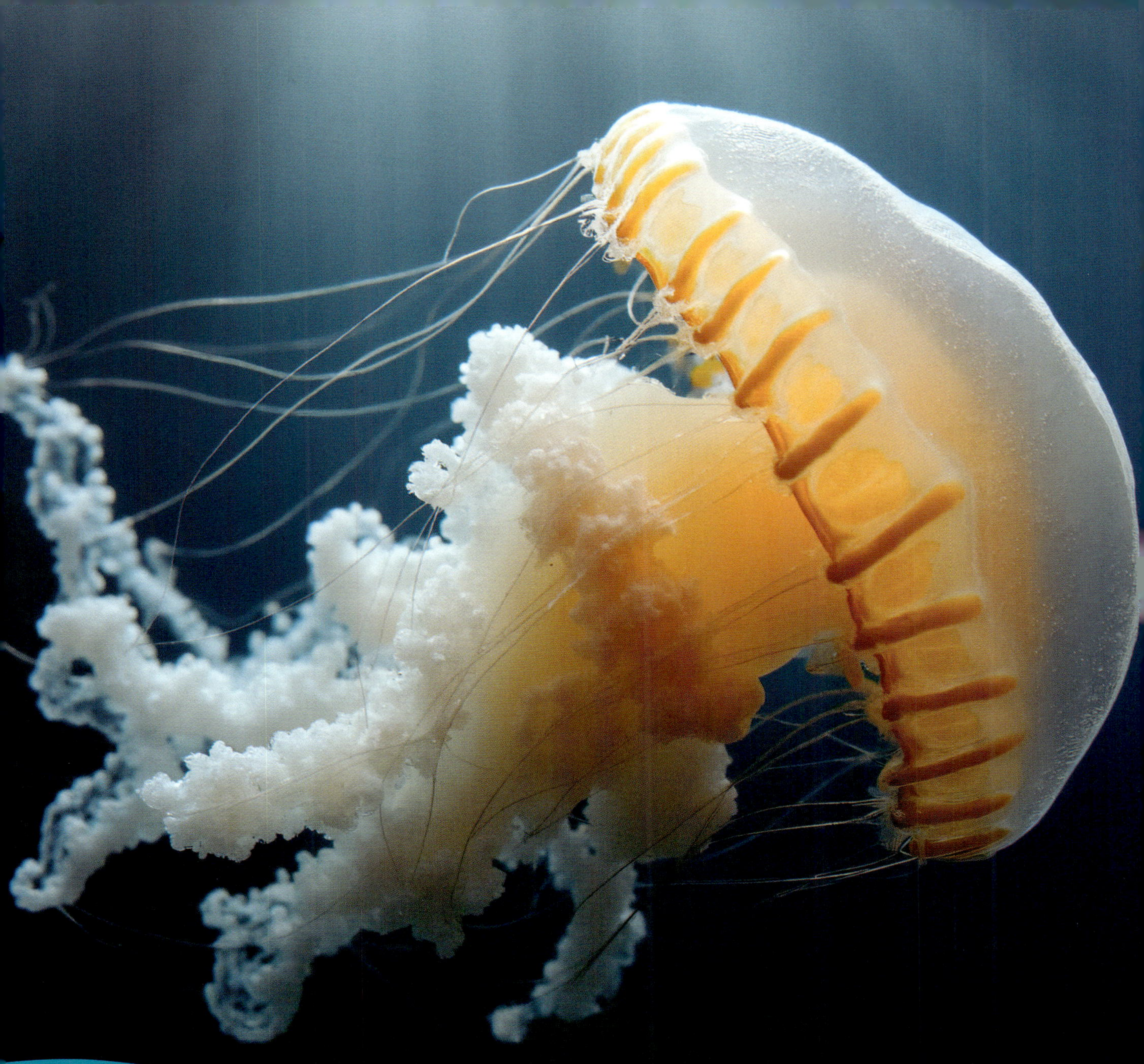

Glossary

barbs (bahrbs): sharp points that stick out and backward; hooks

defend (di-FEND): to protect from danger; to keep enemies away

hives (hives): nests where swarms of bees live

insects (IN-sekts): small animals that have six legs and three body sections and that may have wings

prey (pray): animals eaten by other animals

tentacles (TEN-tuh-kuhls): the long, flexible arms of some animals, such as jellyfish, octopuses, and squid

venom (VEN-uhm): a poison produced by some snakes, spiders, and other animals

victims (VIK-tuhmz): people who get hurt or killed

Thinking Questions

1. What is a barb? What animal has a barbed stinger?
2. Why do fire ants sting?
3. Where is a scorpion's stinger?
4. Why might a stingray sting?
5. Where are a jellyfish's stingers?

Index

barbs 7, 11, 12

defense 6, 10, 14, 19

insects 4, 10–12, 14, 15

prey 6, 20

sharp 4, 17

tails 16, 19

tentacles 20

venom 8

About the Author

Anne Accardi is a librarian who loves reading books and learning new things! She lives in Kansas City, Missouri. When she's not writing, Anne enjoys listening to music, exploring nature around the city, and spending time with her family.